ROBERT
AND THE
MAGIC FOUNTAIN

A 20-PAGE SENSORY-FRIENDLY BOOK

ISABEL MARIE NORTON-LAGO
AND MARK ALAN LITTLE

THIS BOOK IS DEDICATED TO
ROBERT JAMES NORTON

FOREWORD BY ISABEL NORTON-LAGO

"Every journey has its challenges, its moments of despair, but also its rays of hope."

Our journey with Robert started as any other parent's would—with joy, love, and dreams. When Robert was diagnosed with non-verbal autism at 2 1/2 years old, our path took an unexpected turn.

The early days were filled with questions, fears, and the over-whelming desire to connect with our beloved son. Through every therapy session, every tear, and every small milestone, we learned to listen in a different way. We found Robert's voice in his actions, his passions, and the joy he found in simple pleasures.

One of those pleasures was water. The magic of water fountains and their rhythmic dance seemed to resonate with

Robert's soul. It became a bridge, a medium for us to enter Robert's world and for him to share his joy with us.

This book is a celebration of that joy and magic. It's an invitation for every reader to look beyond words, to find connection in actions and shared experiences. It's a testament to our journey, a journey that teaches us every day about love, patience, and the unique beauty of every individual.

To all parents, caregivers, and friends of children with special needs, know that there's always a way, always a bridge. For us, it was a water fountain. For you, it might be something else. Let's find it together.

Love,
Isabel Norton-Lago

Meet Robert Norton, full of fun
and play. With toys all around,
he's happy all day.

He doesn't use words, but with music he's free. Dancing around, as happy as can be.

In the park, kids run and shout.
But the fountain's magic is what
Robert's about.

The water jumps, spins, and twirls. In this fountain, the magic whirls.

Robert feels happy, moving in tune. With the magical water, he's over the moon.

He feels the beat, the music so neat. With the fountain's splash, his joy's hard to beat.

Robert's Jingle

"Magic water, fun and neat,
Dance with me, feel the beat!"

Nature dances too, joining our
friend. With Robert leading,
the fun never ends.

Robert sways with a grin, from one
end to the other. Seeing him joyful,
kids dance with one another.

With magic water and
happy play, Robert lights up
everyone's day.